MALILENAS

Malilenas

ISBN 978-1-933254-58-6

Library of Congress Cataloging-in-Publication Data

Kalleberg, Garrett.
Malilenas / Garrett Kalleberg.
p. cm.
ISBN 978-1-933254-58-6 (pbk. : alk. paper)
I. Title.
PS3561.A41659M36 2009
811'.54--dc22
2009024930

Distributed to the trade by
Small Press Distribution (SPD)
1341 Seventh Street, Berkeley, CA 94710
www.spdbooks.org

Available directly from Ugly Duckling Presse and through our partner bookstores.

This book is made possible in part by generous grants from the National Endowment for the Arts and the Fund for Poetry.

First Edition 2009
Printed in the USA

Ugly Duckling Presse
The Old American Can Factory
232 Third Street, #E-002
Brooklyn, NY 11215

NATIONAL
ENDOWMENT
FOR THE ARTS

www.uglyducklingpresse.org

MALILENAS

Garrett Kalleberg

Ugly Duckling Presse
Brooklyn, 2009

for L

for M

I met two tiny twins
and though they were identical
only one
looked at me

—Ivan Akhmetev

Let the newlyweds be newlyweds in eternity.
So don't strike 1, which will echo into infinity.

—César Vallejo

1.

Sometimes you give me just enough
to live on. Sometimes not.
And like that, from all to nothing,
and still you feed on me.

I've set up a prison in a plastic container that I
put on my windowsill to torture you
with daylight. Then at night can I sleep soundly
and not worry about some number
sucking my blood?

Month 35 since: until there were tens of thousands.

Day minus more: until I couldn't count.

Hour zero and, behind me, already all profits and losses.

2.

A sentence of from now on.
At the end of which a period of endings.

A prisoner,
a prison, and
a notebook—

to extort ambiguity out of language.
As payback for taking meaning out of life—look,
I double my sense and twin my desire

in case I lose one. But how escape?
the imaginary, captive of imagination, the real
a hostage of reality and meaning,
the appearance of significance
or value.
As sentence
the now of the body forever
and over, as payback the passion
of a body for Saturday
take away Friday, as requital
the repetition of bodies as many
and with whom, for love and money.

3.

I am hungry.

I am metaphysical

in the morning. At first light

I grow increasingly
bright and dull, alternately
adding up to alternately
taking away. Then at night

I can *be* hunger and hunger *for* and hunger *of*.

Spiritually starving? Hell, I am
polynomial appetites
and multiplying each one of them will kill each one of them

divided by one
taste of the soul of your sex
or star. *Your* star.

3.

1 times 1.
In the presence of strong attractors
a strange absence occurs.

0 times 0.
Times how many times? how much
is enough? intoxicating end

into which the first stars lunge.
Towards your dim deaths, entelechies.

4.

Something feeds me zeros until
all my energy is consumed
in error correction.
I find myself
on a path I did not ask for
along an arc I cannot prevent.

I cannot prevent arcs.

I cannot prevent paths
in the form of mathematical certainty
or probability.

Something feeds me,
and all my riches are immaterial. No matter
what I have done, or do, or will do,
probability will save me.

5.

Tock tock. Says the clock.
Today is
Happy Day. Affectation. Orgy of Feeling.
And Memory.

Tick tick. The bones of time
broken, click. And judiciously fit
into Common Sense. Imagination. Moral Reason.
And Memory.

Pock pock, by tomorrow
or the day after we'll
find a way out, or
the day after, in. Find
an opening out of closing in, becoming

unhinged. Keep digging,
labor a source of warmth.
Keep moving
into the light, the source, or hole.
And wholly consistent with a gunshot wound.

By morning.......... By morning
the gun was wound up
and alarmed the wound.
The wound woke up

and up!

up

up

6.

Dead in the water and divided by zero
an impossible I rocks gently on the waves
of the fluid curve of a negative movement
which net effect is the cause
of a self-correction trajectory.

Dead it was, and the effect
was reassembled and observations
were made until
it decayed.

It decayed and decayed
and the I passed away
and the water passed away
and the zero passed peacefully away

and all that remained was
free at last of coming or going or
taken from use and become undifferentiated.

7.

The water? What water?
Breaker's wish? Which wish?
Is which's Westron
wind, awash
and list,
wondrous sunset.

Wrecker's beacon. Which
wreck? save our souls. Which the West
beckons away from sea foam
foaming in the dust.
Bottomless, a lust
abounds. Drowned beauty.

Which beauty? small rains.
Which seas' rains down
can rain and suck
souls in and all around
and round and sink
like Spanish gold.

Like the labor of Spanish gold
at gunpoint.

All guns.

Many guns.

8.

Click-click.
As if to empty the room.

Bang-bang.
As if to clean the live chamber.

Snap, snap,
as if every cell

just goes snap. Just my luck
a mutable mute,
I have a clickable brain with enhancer traps.

I am mutants untitled in a knot of hair.

To obtain this state I
call home, call surgeon, finish that letter
to P, but finish, all my hairs, before emptying

into clock speed, alprazolam, seltzer.
Fill the room, my waters,
with just a little bubbles
left OR boolean AND

markup page for daily update:
Monday.
Going on Tuesday.

What are you working on?

Gum. Sugarless gum.

9.

Help me, gum, I am helpless or
less of help and more of gum. Yes,
less yesterday, moreover today and..................
todavía. Vying for a voice

or not really trying at all.
I speak for myself alone.
The hand has played into the hand.
And the mouth swallows its mouth, to Mmm........
And the day after? you too

seemed like a good idea at the time.
Help me, tomorrow. And that Friday
in June? I've always felt bad
about the bad things I've done.

More bad.

Many more.

Many guns and no gum money.

10.

A stream trickles out of my diagram
into five little bodies
borrowed from the nearby.

Do you mind, little bodies? and overflow
into the ground of unknowing
why five? Why not

7   11   13   17   .. little bodies
hanging from the branches of my science
named many.

Ripe, the time passes three, tell me.

Primed, meaning to pass each die
itself and once. I hear you

and each leaf of the fault tree,
indivisible by any number
except one itself
a numberless body.
Invisible by any number, so
we, too, can't be hurt. Hanging

from the branches of the fruitless tree.
Just such luck, to be numb.

Just such luck we are not 19   23   or   29, no
we go on. On and on
the number passes and the leaves,
they're dumb.

11.

The first garden in the god
wrote the leaves of your letter
perverted by language.

The flowers of language seconded
between the prescient loves of your book
wrote poems of trees.

And on the third day
pressed up against writing, preternatural, impassioned
against writing and twisted by an upward eye,
the arm of a downward arm bent rightly
into the fruit of the meaning of the knowledge of
tomorrow.

What did you dream after it happens?
Who will woke with you in your bed?

I wrote what I will
remember folding the page
onto the page after it's not too late.

Lies. All lies.
Advance penance reverses penury.

12.

That the punctuation pinched your arm.
And the black words pulled your black hairs
through the rectangle into the circle.

Then the closure close to re-opening
uncomfortably around the idea of being
became a terminal dot.

You did not come through. You came. I went. It went
like this:

A misplaced comma,
an unmatched parenthesis, an error
in spelling, or worse, calling an object
without first instantiating the object.
And it all comes crashing down,
or worse, that it, the poem *works*

but an incorrect result is produced.
Then who will pay the price for this?
Who can put a price on this?

$28 left and still no euphoria.

13.

Mimicked, mocked, magnificent.
What makes me many
makes me want.

Mimicked, inimical, individual.
What makes many me
makes you wonder.
And makes me want you.

What makes me makes
sense, and thought, and feeling
I'm asking you,
am I so manipulated
to get it?

What?

What what?

And when it is had or done, call it
destiny, fate, or meaning. I'll pay and
why not? if only I had the money.

14.

The hard share and necessity have
bloodied my lines with the blood
of other people's words. No easy share
to write, in joint misery snatched
and dispatched by hands
penned behind the back.

No easy trick, I'd say.
No easy way out, violence voiced by pens
gnawing into our little notebooks—Sorry
we are that we can say no more.

Sorry, blood, sorry, salt,
It's always about the money.

Sorry spittle on lipstick of spasming
lips, *Just go.* The language spent in excess
even the breath broke

look

a poet's corpus.

A palaver cadavers.

15.

I'm worried about you,
she said. Your word is empty, your letters
have no form.

I'm concerned about you, it scares me
when you talk like that.
You don't open your mouth, the sound
does not come out.

What happens to the sound, closed in.
What happens to the word, closed in the mouth.

The words, I like meeting new people, closed up.
The words, You have a nice beard—I have white too, she,
bending down her head, are closed up.
The words, Sara, with an h, Sarah with the wet hands, will be
closed up.

16.

Look at the truth in beauty—
how it squirms and wriggling
feeds off decay's disseminating
decadence but oddly

has no smell, the poem,
and unevenly forms a form
of life and so
alive and so

I must kill it.
I get bored, you know, I kill it, and you,

do you still take pleasure
in the game? in principle wording words

into quiescence.
To write is to kill the word
and fix it into place, Peace

Peace
unto all ye words

now no one can hour you.
And minutely ye,
days and secondly ye

of all times—ye
not yet.

17.

To be inexactly 0
from minus to plus
but stopping in maturity at the discharge
of all charges.

Oscilla between negation and apposition.

To be, more or less
or at least for the pregnant moment
if not in this cafe
in this not cafe not.

0 wriggling lively at the edge of a culture.

To be inexactly 0
hence detectable, the yes is apposite the yes
as the no is no. Sitting in the cafe like a poet
on the verge of poetastisizing.

Or what is a prediction if it can't be proved wrong?

To be is to have,
and to have is to have passion, or
to be is to not have, or be
an apposition between
adding up to, and amounting to—

or what is a poem if it can't be interpreted wrong?

Or how the scintilla scintillates............

Heavy with the children of meaning.

18.

The unpronounceable key word
at sullen fingertips turns silently
into more locks.
My good hand is forever
and ever entering into

or among the mysteries of being
without. Without
opening and without closing and
without being

inside. And if, give or take, the word
opens—like the prodigal home? Into every house
I enter, I bring baggage

of doors. Pure passage. Knock
at my fingertips.

19.

The diseased hand in the good hand
holds the pen.

The good hand in the diseased hand
holds the book.

The book holds the bilious inks
in a book called Bile.

It is a good book
and good bile even so
unable to relinquish spleen.

And the ink squishing in the word
unable to discharge of all debts the good
hand that put it there.

20.

A good notebook is the mother of the muses.

The notebook is the mother.

The writer who keeps a lover, the writer in love,
is one who cannot give up happiness
or the satisfaction of days that are really days.
And the lovers that succeed one another.

Dear N,

I give up. I forfeit. I
in resignation forswear, I
in resignation abandon. With my signature

and initials here, here, and here I
let go, lay down, with all signs I
throw away, aside, behind me. I cast off
to the dogs, to the winds I capitulate
my capitals and castigate the lower cases

of my lower lovers and the higher lovers
and all the relative others burning
in levity and turning

in their gravity. Cursive
mothers in levity father
words in gravity good
notebook in levity
blessed.

21.

No matter how hard I tried
I couldn't withdraw the word
from the page, the one word
I was looking for.

The word wasn't cleared by the ink
—you saw the look on my face.
The ink identified the hand and the hand
put a hold on the book. For what it's worth,

we'll go over and back again and
cross these crooked lines
and uncross thricefold thrice.
No matter the one and

the one minus the capital
investment in past mistakes.
No matter my income or outcome,
all is fair. And for now, we're even.

I see the look on your face.

21.

So tell me,
what does principle cost you?
How much of the other's share
are you willing to lose? The upside
to risk is not the side
facing you and, at the bottom,
I can see you're not smiling.

I can hear your lips moving,
so tell me,
what does the word cost you?
Either say it's worth the pain or
is pain, I'm asking you, tell me,

tell me what to do.
I am vested in interest and
have my own principles,
and you
who owns me

who?
Say something.

Say what you have to say, dude, but be yourself,
whatever you do
follow your heart and

your lips

your tongue.

22.

Nothing can go out if it doesn't come in.

Nothing good can enter in if it doesn't leave something else.

And in a little while, just leave

by the nearest exit. I'm asking you,
IN CASE OF FIRE USE STAIRCASE.

In case of death, go to heaven.
I'll make a fire in your eyes—

and for that desire that burns, leave
one door open.
And one door closed.

Prepare yourself for judgement, or be closed.

22.

With no way out and up against the wall
I'll encrypt my keys.

Open yourself for rebuke or ready yourself for worse.

With blades, pincers, a camera for arms
or legs, I'll
enter your body through a keyhole

or port, I will
entice your body through a keyhole
until the whole of your being is locked up.

I am the key
said Peter. And I am the lock
said I.

23.

The wind comes in
through a small hole. The word comes in
through a small hole. Through a small hole
I can hear you calling,

Come in.
The door is open.

Is the door open?
in reality.
Is someone coming in?
in reality.

No, I said, he is not
in reality.

And the wind the door the hole
grew smaller and closed
until we lost her.

24.

The key turned in the lock.
The blade turned in the wound.
Time turned in the clock.
And meaning, turned 'round, was found.

Ha ha!

. . .

The sign reassigned and
something alive, good luck
with what to live for,
should the poem, too, sound

productive of mood
contrive delusion in the wound
as the surgery has
produced the illness

accommodating the pain?
Speaking plainly, I'm arrived
and bound, no turning back
with you or without you,

your turn. No reason to be down,
let me see your pain
and I'll show you mine.
Now it's your turn

said the ghostly whole
stripped of dignity.
Now it's your turn,
said the phantom pain

naked before the after.
Now it's your turn,
said the human spirit
brown-eyed, smiling

and naked of human spirit.
Now it's your turn.

Ha ha!

25.

Collect & recollect
yet never settle
nor account for the self
reckoned.

In preparation, reconcile
all accounts with all
losses, no less the account
of reconciliation.

However err, err
in twos with no
investment on the return
of one.

I cannot withdraw the word
come to maturity
nor dissent of asset
trading out futures

with all my assonance seized
and constantly consonance
echoes cataclysmic economy.

26.

And set to war
with myself, to ally
with myself, to advance
the cause of myself
in spite of myself, an otherwise
peace-loving man,

Onward! all my men.
Forward! into the future poem
of voices
in advance of—.

The next sound you hear will be
~~the sound of your own voice~~.
I scratch
an irritation of regressions
and progress in corrections
in advance of looking
back at the ass of progress.

26.

And everything I read.

To war
with itself, the poem—
Forward! all my men.
Onward, chiasmic soldiers. Turn
and fight.

It is a good war
and a good fight and
we shall pay any price.
Bear any burden. Or our words
bankrupt, no longer able to bear
the weight of an argument.

Advance lightly, then,
armored in a sign, in writing
towards only one outcome, goal, or end:
that everything is lost, forgotten.

And stand. *Destructions are come*
to a perpetual end.

27.

I'm glad we met,
says the joy of fucked-up luck
to a beautiful disaster.

In regards to which beauty, wounded,
remains silent.

I can't speak, I've been trying to tell you—
too late to get into that again.
I'm just happy you're here.

You came and
you're here and here is here and

there is oblivion misinterpreted
as metaphysical. I lose myself

but am happy
I found you
repeatedly and I
myself but
happy
you
and
at a cruel rate,
accrual.

27.

Destitute of worth, having no value.

Destitute of words, having no significance.

Though I meant what I said and
wrote and, writing off
the wreck and the reckoner

cash out in the everyday.
What a beautiful accident! Can I say that?
That's life, she said.

Capitalize on past mistakes and still you
need a good business sense.
A calculated risk, a cultivated loss—
form a bond with abandon

all you bonds, form
and be content. For whom
and how many

and how many times you begin again
depends on how many times you end.

27.

I'd rather beauty wreck me than
only dream of having it.
And when I wake up remember

the others you love, and I love,
—be fair. Be kind. Take care
of the things in your life.

And I, mine. Fairness a thing
the others dreamt up
so they know what they have.

28.

Thank you for the book
in which every accident is predestined
as need, condemned to repeat
the initial conditions
in an initial C.

Which also Contains the sCene of the last judgement
and in ConClusion
as it was transCribed, so was he Condemned.

They will love you when you're dead, she said.

And I will love you, too, he said.

He tied his boot. Then his other boot.
Now he has two boots tied!

Boy at the sCene of an aCcident in an initial C.

29.

For gain of insight I invested all I had
in yet another insight, no end
to the riches of labor, as long as I live.

So I can give you some time
inasmuch as I have time to give.
And someday meet again as lovely strangers
with no end to beginning

past the future become bad timing.
And wait. Wait,
save yourself
or save me, though I don't bank on intention
nor trust in guarantee
nor agree on what things mean

in case, number or gender
meaning
well
with what I had.
Not an easy loss not
much at all.

In reparation for which I'd honor a debt
in seeing to another's interests
dishonored by the other's interests—
you think it's easy for me? but now
I'm off the grid, column, row, and cell.

Free? to my credit, all my riches
are immaterial, no matter
the mind minting
counterfeit affections enough

to buy a treasury of trust
whose notes bear no significance
compared to what buys a glass of beer.

Free? at least without the measure
of chapter and verse even then
something to pay for.

At least love.

30.

Would you like another? he said.

I would be happier by one third,
I said.

And by a fourth?
then by a fifth
of happiness but never
a whole number.

I divide by imaginary happinesses
until (this requires a blackboard's patience
and scientific chalk, which I don't have having
no number or quantity)
when the fact of then thens,
I will have two facts.

Adding up to half-life
decaying into see-through
self-image, in a cup,
just the way I like it.

Half-of-love
frozen in time, strange
frigidity of the beautiful
in a cup, just the way I like it.

Half-plate, what is love?
in a cup, just the way I like it.

Half a third, cool
half a fourth, hot
then a fraction of whole milk
in-a-cup, just the way I like it.

31.

Dopamine
disencumbers much craving
euphoria &
much craving. But true pleasure

the Opioids
time pleasures. Time
pleasures and opens like
an opening also, also
lessens the pain. But true happiness

Serotonin
balances   well-being
in a balance. More than that,

Neural Growth Factors
of affective organization in
migration, differentiation, programmed death
produce the euphoria
of love and dependency.

Dopamine.

32.

You have beautiful eyes,
I said to the mirror.
This was the day I went blind.

I like to watch,
said the mirror.
This was the day I tore my eyes out.

Unable to see,
my hearing became quite acute
give me this

and I heard a voice say,
Who are you talking to?
And when I opened my eyes,

¡Mira! how good we look together!
Even now, one says, I will follow you,
imaginary friend, into the future,

then is gone. Now only one of us
in the mirror.
The mirror says,
I will follow you, imaginary friend,
into the future, then is gone.
Now no one, nothing left to prove I'm smiling.

33.

In the male, the female.
And in the familial a blank check

signed by all signs, backed
by the capital of all signifieds,

fronted by the signifier in all things.
We can do anything

discharged of all debts, banished
from all trespasses, obviated

in all obligations
and tied to no tie nor three-button coat,

not manacled to the man of the manual man
nor exactly seared onto the soul of the cerebral man,

just don't buy those boots you saw with Serena
and make the sandwich endure lunch unto supper.

33.

Something to profit in.
In all things are numbers.

As everything for something and
all for nothing. A transaction

in which everyone is happy.
Having what they know they have.

I have something for you, is
a known unhappiness better

than an unknown happiness?
And you, what you want.

Who shall take it away?
Give me something to believe in,

or what shall it profit a man
lest he profits?

34.

The sun moved:
it's 3:05 PM—money in the bank!
Spent by 3:07 trying to hold on to 3:06.
Thank you for having been there.

It doesn't matter how much the gross deficit is
as long as we have continued growth
and preferential detachment.
Spreading through every body.
My skin skins
from within, and outside, my art
grows a growth of formlessness.
My tongue poetastisizes, that's what I do
but now try to say it. In this way
it's less painful to write than to not
remain silent.

Whereof, write
poem, spread throughout. And grow therein.
And in th'air, in your hair and skin.

35.

Between the devil and the damned
is someone making a profit?

It doesn't matter if we're separated
by geography or asset class,

we trade together in corrections
with hell to pay and from heaven

the gift of the debt of gratitude.

36.

It's almost 9:57 AM.
You can hold out, beauty.
You can hold on with those sexy incisors

mouthing desire, teething affection,
you can survive—I'm a survivor! you said
—another day. Be patient.

It's 5:57 PM. Almost.
No time to lose, now
—give in. Yes! Just like that?

Give up now, beauty!
Break down, all teeth,
break all lips and tongues

into the smallest digestible units.
And coat these units with sugar-glass.
I read an article, but can't remember what it's called, anyway.

It's the day after tomorrow
almost. Be patient. It happens. Beauty survives.
Well, wait until the next infusion of cash

until you, even the littlest bits
of beauty unsweeten into life, flow
into and all over—again? *Again!* Eat me alive.

37.

While the months divided us
the years multiplied the months. And now?
Only a few days separate us. Then?
Then hours. Then?
Then minutes. Then?
Then seconds. Then milliseconds. Then microseconds. Then nanoseconds.

Nano.

Nano, why do you come between us?

Na na no.
Na no.

Na na.

No na no.

Na na.

Na.

38.

No. Don't speak of the years.
Don't give me that shit, *the time passes*, was that
Anno Mirabilis? 2005
Anno Domini? from the miraculous
anuses of God.

Don't tell me about how many
many was, or is, or will be,
this year almost over, thank God
anno annulled miraculously and
nulla dies sine linea.

Liar. Yes,

let's not speak of words or
from or with or in words, let's
take them out and
line them all up till they form a line.

And scratch them off one at a time
until all that's left is

you

alone a line.

Let's not
speak of the years. Even the months
were against us, and the weeks,

and the days, especially
a week ago Friday.

39.

As proof, of the possible:
how you smiled at me.

As proof, of position:
I was your prisoner.

You are like my prisoner! you said.
You called my name.

You brought me an apple.

You brought me a pitcher of water,
and tamarind candy.
You gave me a place to sleep, and dream, and love
on the bed, until I couldn't move.

When you let me go, you told me
everything was going to be okay one day.
Did I have any choice but to obey you, and go?

Tell me what to do! you said.

40.

Despair in dissembling more.
Delusion in afterlife library.
Dollar in one dollar pocket.

Something here................
Something to work with.
At least work.

From dissemblance, remembrance
deluded of dollars and
nothing left to give. Given

desire, a garden in rainy season and birds
of paradise, purge
all desire. From labor, at least increasing

the knowledge you now know
what decrease dissembles.
At least labor.

41.

A second hand and a minute chance
revive hope of probability or
improbability equally.

And this hour, however poorly situated
as result of a wholesale revelation,
however artistically gifted

an unenviable reversal of fortune,
however in verse, enticed, the turn,
an encumbered remembrance

remembers encumbrance. And counterturn,
the properties of money being this for that.

42.

I wanted to come back
to the place I came from but
when I arrived they told me
you are here.
And the place I came from no longer existed.

That's when I knew I'd come back
for you again and again and
for a moment you
just have to hold on for the moment.

I wanted to come back
to the place I came from
but when I arrived I knew
you came back, too, to say good-bye.

Worse comes to worst.
Restless the worser,
and still the end. Just
show up, and show up good. The end,
by any account, will be well arrived.

43.

Extravagance by extravagance.
Dollar by dollar.
Every string pulled from me so that I'm finally free.

I'm an intellectual vagrant.
I'm a waste of money. Yes,
but by the end of next week your soul will be pure, she said.

Number by number.
Mother by mother.
Hair by hair, until I'm free.

Does this count? Finally,
new minuses and new plusses.

44.

¡Por favor! because you like it.
¡Por favor! ¡Por favor! because you want it.
¡Por favor! because you can,
                                        —use the bookcase
as a ladder, after all there's
nowhere else to go
but up
          and up
                    into the upper
limits of literature,

watch your head! Alright,
I'm going! Up
to the upper. Down
to the lower, and increasingly
low down. Until bottommost, let me

rest here, shorter or longer, like glue
to the one with none remaining—climber
of intellectual consonants, vertiginist
of emotive vowels, tongue of p-p-p-p-

tongues and
Mouth! Counter-squeak!

45.

Give the writer love.

Love absent, give the writer hope.

Hope absent, give the writer something,
something to do.

So I write: The only difference between true
and false hope is that the false is
less likely to increase disappointment.

. . .

Write love. Love
unreadable, write hope.
Hope illegible,
taking writing for saying,
say something, write anything.

Set up a table, open a new notebook.

Write this down: event # E01632209
if you have a purpose in this system. Otherwise,
please go down to Room 156.

Always a back door. Leave

always a back door.

An escape plan.

Boxes.

46.

Tonight, in a cantina down Bolívar, there's one color TV and two black and white waiters. And one pale finger between the folds of a book.

Tomorrow, or *esotro día*, there will be a book to touch a place within our folds. So we, too, have something to say. There has to be.

Tomorrow or *esotro día,* something must touch us, in the way the pen, or the glass can't help it, or the table itself—Table! Say something!

Tonight, talk to me, or *esotra noche.* The table is going nowhere. Pinned by a formidable elbow calloused by innumerable pinnings. Even the book doesn't have a chance, splayed—Face down! Don't move!

Even the image of a woman, annunciate, her pale fingers in the folds of a book must bow her head, eyes closed,—and her lips—.

Come, you said, holding me in ways until I could no longer move.

Go, you said—did you mean *Let go*, or *Go on, don't stop!* or *Go away?*

Come, you said, and I was more than ready! I was *almost*.

Don't come, you said.

And you—table? Just as I thought. But even if you could, who'd believe what you said?

47.

I am going.
I cannot go.
I am glued to the one

with three remaining.
Left. Right. And overhead.
If you can call it "head,"

says mouth. I'm quitting this country
and taking my conscious man and
animal nature with me.

I'm really getting on the plane.
I'm leaving the hotel now....

I'm walking out of the room, "King Size," $28. And
in front of me, closing,
an opening! An opening, closing! also

behind me.
5:32. First light
any minute now.

Fuck. A bed squeaks.

Notes and Acknowledgements:

Ivan Akhmetev epigraph, trans. Alex Cigale.

César Vallejo epigraph, from *Trilce*, trans. Clayton Eshleman.

Poems beginning "The diseased hand in the good hand" and "A good notebook is the mother of the muses" are variations on themes in Maurice Blanchot's essay translated variously in English as "The Essential Solitude."

Poem beginning "And everything I read."—"We shall pay any price, bear any burden" is from JFK; "destructions are come to a perpetual end" is from Psalm 9.

Thanks to Dan Machlin, Laird Hunt, Eleni Sikelianos, and Matvei Yankelevich. Thanks to the Fund for Poetry for saving my life, twice. And thanks to Laura Solórzano, to whom this book is lovingly dedicated.

Thanks to the editors of *Eleven Eleven*, *Action, Yes*, and *La Inquietante (e Internacional) Semana de las Mujeres Traducidas* in which sections of this book also appeared.

Garrett Kalleberg's previous volumes of poetry include *Some Mantic Daemons*, *Psychological Corporations*, and *Limbic Odes*. His poetry, reviews, and translations have appeared in various journals, including *Brooklyn Rail*, *Fence*, *Denver Quarterly*, and *American Letters & Commentary*. Garrett's theatrical work *The Situation Room* was produced by Brooklyn Drama Club for Collective Unconscious, New York, 2002, and The New York International Fringe Festival, 2003. From 1998 to 2002, Garrett edited *The Transcendental Friend* and the Immanent Audio label. His awards for poetry and critical writing include grants from Poets & Writers, the Academy of American Poets, and the Fund for Poetry.

This first edition, consisting of 900 copies, was printed and bound at McNaughton and Gunn (Saline, Michigan), into Fabriano Tiziano covers offset printed at Polyprint Design (New York City) and letterpressed at the Ugly Duckling Presse workshop (Brooklyn, New York). An additional 40 copies, bound into special covers with hand-set titles, were numbered and signed by the author.

Malilenas was designed by Will Hubbard. Titles are set in Futura Condensed, and the text in Garamond 3.